Living Music Box...

(U. S. Patent No. 50853)

is the registered name of a special strain of St. Andreasberg Roller Canaries, especially bred for us in Germany and directly imported by us and therefore absolutely unobtainable from other dealers. It is the most wonderful trained singing canary in the world, the bird you have heard so much talk about.

Beware of Imitators

In order to protect ourselves and our patrons, we have registered in the Patent Office of the United States our Geisler-Roller Canaries, under the name of "Living Music Box." This name must be stamped on the inside wing of each bird as well as on its shipping cage.

None Genuine
Without This Stamp

If you are looking for something extra fine in the line of Canaries, order one of these birds and you will never regret it. Thousands of unsolicited testimonials from all parts of the United States and foreign countries on hand. Write for free Bird book. It is free for the asking.

❑ ❑ ❑

For Prices See Page 10 of this
Catalogue.

Max Geisler Bird Co.

ILLUSTRATED CATALOGUE

IMPORTERS OF AND DEALERS IN

Birds, Fancy Fish, Dogs, Rare Animals, Cages, Aquariums, Globes, Shells, Etc.

RETRO PEACOCK EDITION, 1931-1932
INTRODUCTION by R. PEACOCK

Published in 2010 by Retro Peacock Books
Toronto, Canada
www.RetroPeacock.com

This book was originally published as an illustrated catalogue and price
list in 1931 by Max Geisler Bird Company of Omaha, Nebraska.

To stay informed about upcoming Retro Peacock editions, please visit
www.RetroPeacock.com.

Printed in the United States of America

First edition

ISBN-13: 978-1-45-150709-6
ISBN-10: 1-45-150709-7

INTRODUCTION

Dear Reader,

Indulging in mementos of the past can be a magical experience which brings a certain yearning a foregone world which is fanciful and free of the intricacies of modern life. Consider, for example, a time as recently as the turn of the twentieth century when people lived in a world where wild birds and exotic animals were thought of as abundantly available commodities to be freely kept as pets. These animals were commodified to such an extent that one could open up a mail-order catalogue and select pets sold under trademarked brand names. Buying a pet was as easy and as routine as browsing through a catalogue for furniture, toys, and items for the home.

In fact, there were many intriguing companies which sold pets to consumers using the mail-order model of business. In the 1930s, one of the most popular distributors was **Max Geisler Bird Company**, self-touted as the "Largest and Oldest Mail Order Bird House in the World." Founded in 1888, this company was a pioneer and leader in the mail-order pet industry, importing animals from around the world and shipping to customers all over Canada, Mexico, and the United States.

This book offers fascinating glimpse of the many birds and other exotic fancy which were available as pets to all who could afford them. Offerings from Max Geisler Bird Co. were highlighted by their signature, trademarked lines of pet birds: the "Human Talker" parrots which were guaranteed to learn to talk, and the "Living Music Box," a strain of St. Andreasberg Roller Canaries described as "a little song wonder." Beyond these, the company offered a menagerie of other exotic creatures available for order, including Flamingos, Marmozette Monkeys (the smallest monkey in existence), the large and silky Angora cat, novelty Japanese Dancing mice for young children, chameleons, Chinese Telescope Goldfish, and even Burmese Peacocks!

This high-quality edition is a faithful replication of the original catalogue produced in 1931, using a rare original source copy. **Retro Peacock** is dedicated to producing fine quality art and photo editions of ornithological ephemera utilizing modern digital imaging methods, and all of our editions have been expertly processed to capture all the details of the original. Every tiny stroke of the many etchings included in this volume has been detailed and reproduced. Recreated using technology far superior to any available in 1931, this catalogue is printed and optimized for maximal quality and longevity in a format that captures the appearance of the original catalogue when first printed.

Whether you are a pet-lover, a collector of ephemera, a historian, or an afficiando of vintage literature, this book will be an excellent addition to your collection and enable you to experience and relive what were once bygone memories of the past.

We Hope That You Will Enjoy This Book

> **R. Peacock**
> RetroPeacock.com

SOME SCENES OF OUR TRANSPORTS

A 25 foot Python Snake on "S. S. Orient" from India.

Unloading one of our Elephants from a truck.

Taking care of 1800 Canaries on board the "S. S. Berlin" from Germany.

SOME FACTS ABOUT OUR IMPORT BUSINESS

We import about 100,000 Canaries every year to New York besides thousands of Foreign Birds, Fancy Fowls and Animals; from a Marmozette (the smallest monkey in existence) to an Elephant.

We have our own Collectors in Calcutta and Singapore (India) Bahia and Para (Brazil), Leon (Nicaragua), also Columbia, Africa and other foreign countries. In Europe we have our own buyers, Marseilles (France), London and Norwich (England), Rotterdam (Holland), Antwerp (Belgium) and our own Import House in Hannover (Germany).

All these Birds, with exception of our special strain of "Living Music Box" canaries are sold at wholesale to Bird Dealers all over in U. S. A., the animals to Animal Dealers, Zoos and Show People.

During the season we have fifteen men on the water continuously between Hamburg and New York, bringing over transports of Canaries. Each man has to take care of about 1500 birds.

More Than One Hundred Thousand Birds Imported Annually

From Our European Headquarters

To Our New York Headquarters

We erected this building in Hannover, Germany in 1922. Its 32 rooms are devoted entirely to the assembling and housing of canaries and foreign birds.

This is our New York import house. Prominent Zoological Directors have named these four floors "The most Sanitary Import House in the East."

Preparing a shipment of Canaries for transportation from our Hannover House in Germany to our New York House. Each crate contains 210 birds in separate wooden cages. A bird man who accompanies each transport takes care of about 1500 birds while enroute.

OUR WAREHOUSE
Omaha

Max Geisler
Prop. Max Geisler Bird Company

ANNOUNCEMENT
SEASON 1931-1932
All Prices Subject to Change Without Notice

IN PRESENTING herewith our new catalogue to our patrons we wish to express the desire that it may fulfill the purpose for which it has been written, namely, in assisting you to make a selection of an article which will give entire satisfaction and at the same time be a credit to our house. It will show you in word and picture a line of goods which will always be appreciated by everyone, young or old, man or woman, and not being expensive it will also be within the reach of everyone. Our quotations are F. O. B. Omaha, or F. O. B. New York City, and the lowest for first-class stock. Our aim has always been to give entire satisfaction to our customers, and to judge from the thousands of unsolicited, sometimes very flattering letters from our patrons from all parts of the U. S., Canada, Mexico and other foreign countries, we believe that we have been very successful in our efforts.

Every single bird, fish, etc., is carefully inspected before packed and not forwarded unless in perfect, sound and healthy condition. All goods are shipped at buyer's risk, but our approved method of packing entitles us to assert that we can ship birds, etc., any distance in the United States, Canada and Mexico with perfect safety. Losses, if any, we always try to adjust to the entire satisfaction of our patrons. We save our customers unnecessary express charges by forwarding at the lowest rate, in extra light shipping cages, etc., which we do not make any charge for, but we expect the same to be returned immediately, free of all charges. Express charges for returning empties are only 15 cents per cage, if returned by the same company that forwarded it. Although our terms are cash with order, we will, if preferred, send goods C. O. D. If enough money accompanies the order to cover express charges both ways. The best method of sending money is by Express, Postal Money Order or Bank Draft; for small amounts up to $1.00, postage stamps (wrapped in wax paper) will be accepted, but never send personal checks, as this causes delay of order and an additional expense of 15c, which is charged by banks for exchange.

One more very important word: Every business no matter what kind, requires some confidence from its patrons, but none to such an extent as the dealing in birds and other live stock, and we are sorry to admit the fact that many unscrupulous bird dealers very often, are taking advantage of this by sending their customers inferior stock, which, as they very well know, would otherwise soon die and be a loss on their own hands or they will sell you a "trapped" parrot, which will never learn to talk, as a "hand raised" one, guaranteeing him as a "good talker," or birds which never sing as "good singers," or females for males, etc. Therefore be careful who you are dealing with, and only trust your order in someone's hands who is worthy of your confidence; only order of an established firm, whose long existence in business gives you a security that you will be treated right and honestly. We guarantee our stock to be as represented, or money will be refunded. We have no agent or agencies, but our seed, food and medicines may be procured from any reliable druggist, grocer or pet dealer in U. S. or Canada, (See page 48.)

The fact that we have been in business here in Omaha for the past 40 years and the many entirely unsolicited testimonials given here in this book and on separate sheet, of which the original, besides thousands of others can be seen by calling at our office, may assure you that we are worthy of your confidence.

MAX GEISLER BIRD CO.

References: U. S. National Bank of Omaha, or Corn Exchange Bank, Astor Place, N. Y. City.

TALKING PARROTS

We make a specialty of young, hand-raised Parrots, which we import in large quantities direct from Mexico, Panama and Brazil, and which we therefore are able to sell at a lower price than any other dealer in the United States, considering quality. We give a written guarantee with every young Parrot to learn to talk within six months; and in case of failure (which hardly ever happens) we agree to exchange without any extra charge. If you intend to buy a good Parrot, in fact, the best in existence, we advise you to order a young hand-raised, "Mexican Double Yellow-headed Parrot," or a "Panama," also called "The Human Talkers," because they imitate the human voice to perfection, and their talking ability is unlimited. They can also be easily taught to sing and whistle. They are considered among bird fanciers as the best talkers in the world, and in fact there is none better. If you want to buy a cheap Parrot, we can recommend either a young, hand-raised "Mexican Red-headed" Parrot, which kind is especially noted as becoming great pets, or a "Pine Island" Parrot. When ordering a Parrot be sure to order at the same time a supply of seed and food. In case you cannot obtain same in your town, if you will send us the name of a reliable druggist we will see if we can make arrangements with him to carry our preparations in stock. Full directions how to take care of, feed and train a young Parrot, will be sent with every bird. Directions for the care of grown Parrots will be found printed on the back of our Parrot Seed boxes, and also on page 61 of this catalogue.

A Few Letters Showing How Well Our Patrons Are Pleased With Our "Human Talker."

Mrs. B. E. Schoppenhorst, Clay City, Indiana, writes: "For some time I have been wanting to write you in regard to 'Human Talker'—Panama parrot—I received from you one year ago last June. He is now some over two years old, and he is a wonder, to say the least. He is the greatest pet I think we have ever had and we have had a number of pets. We call him "Max" and he sure knowns his name. I would like to tell you the many things he says and sings but I will give you some of the list. No one has trained him but myself. He doesn't swear or use bad language of any kind and wont as long as he is mine. He sings the chorus to our high school song which is: 'Well, it's hip, hip, high, dear old Clay City High, Throw your colors, bright and free. So where'er we go, you will always know that we're for you, Old Clay City High.' Another bit from a little song: 'Howdy, howdy, howdy-do, up there in the sky, I am well, how are you up there in the sky.' He calls my husband, my daughter, her husband, the two dogs by name and early in the morning he talks so nice and good, something like this; 'Pretty bird! pretty birdie. You're pretty, you're so pretty; you are; **sure, sure.**' 'Are you all right, huh? What's the matter old top? Are you hungry? Are you cold? 'Come on, that's the time.' 'Do you want your head rubbed?' (he is fond of having his head rubbed so of course we have said this to him). 'Come on, let's whistle, and he whistles too). 'You're a sight!' 'Clay City, Clay City, rah, rah, rah!' 'Gingle bells, gingle bells, gingle all the way,' 'Hello, Aunt Belle,' 'Cut it out,' 'Max quit that,' and 'What's you doin'.'"

"Well, in all he has 89 words in his vocabulary and he keeps learning more all the time. So I want to thank you over and over again for him. We wouldn't take double the price paid for him, and he is perfectly healthy and happy.

MAX GEISLER BIRD CO., OMAHA, NEB. AND NEW YORK CITY

Panama Parrot   Mexican Double Yellow Head

OUR SPECIALTY
"THE HUMAN TALKER"

These Parrots are a SPECIAL SELECTION from hundreds of our own Importations of "Mexican Double Yellow Heads" and "Panama" Parrots. They give such wonderful satisfaction as a talker, that our customers have named them rightly the "Human Talker." They are large sized birds of a beautiful bright green plumage, red and blue feathers in wings and tail. The Mexican has a yellow forehead, the Panama has a gold yellow spot on neck when full grown.

Mexican Double Yellow Heads—During July and August.......$18.00
    Later in the season, $20.00 to $25.00.

Panamas—During season $20.00
    Later in the season, $25.00 to $30.00.

Each Parrot is sold with a written guarantee to learn to talk within 6 months.

A choice selection of above Parrots which will make exceptional good talkers are $5.00 higher. Most of these Parrots are already beginning to talk.

Mrs. M. Woodall, 110 West Main Street, Starkville, Miss., writes: "I am sending for polly another dozen of Parrit Seed so please send at once. I was looking over your book of directions how to make polly talk, so if my polly keeps up his talking you will have to send me word how to keep him from talking all the time. I've heard three people say, I would get a parrot if I knew he would be as smart as yours, I told them that you had just as smart parrots as mine, so I think you will get some orders in the near future. My parrot is a wonderful advertisement for your house, he has a human voice, mine is a Panama Parrot and is just beautiful, you couldn't buy him at any price.

MAX GEISLER BIRD CO., OMAHA, NEB. AND NEW YORK CITY

Mexican Red-headed Parrots—A fair talker, gentle disposition. Medium in size, nice green plumage with a bright red forehead, red and blue feathers in wings and tail.
Price during July and August...................................$ 8.00
    Later in the season, $9.00 to $10.00.

Pine Island Parrots—A fair talker, easy to teach. Medium size, green plumage, each feather nicely black seamed, with bright red breast, red and blue feathers in wings and tail and white forehead.
Price during July and August...................................$ 8.00
    Later in the season, $9.00 to $10.00.

African Gray Parrots—Very rare, as good a talker as the Mexican or Panama. Large size, nice gray plumage, with bright red tail $75.00

Single Yellow-headed Parrots—Good talkers. Medium in size, plumage same as Double Yellow-heads, only the yellow on top of head does not extend so far back.........................$18.00

Blue-fronted Amazon Parrots—Good fair talkers. Same size and plumage as Single Yellow-head, but blue instead of a yellow forehead $18.00

IMPORTANT NOTICE

Above quotations are for **young hand-raised,** tame Parrots in first-class condition, most all already commencing to talk or talking a little.
We give a written guarantee with every young Parrot to learn to talk within six months.
We herewith beg to call to your attention the following:
There are two distinctions to be made in Parrots, namely: **hand-raised** and **trapped** Parrots. The first refers to **young** birds taken out of the nest and raised by hand (hand-raised). These will always learn to talk, will learn rapidly and easily and turn out excellent talkers; are tame and hardy. The latter refers to Parrots caught wild (trapped), which will never learn to talk, never get tame, and as a rule never do well in captivity for any length of time.
Remember, if you want a talker, always order a **hand-raised** bird.
There are sometimes Mexican Double Yellow-headed Parrots offered by unreliable dealers or peddlers as young hand-raised birds, warranted to talk, at prices which to furnish a hand-rasied bird for is impossible. Of course those are trapped Parrots, generally very old and of no value whatever, as they will never learn to talk. We keep a few of them on hand merely to show the difference to our customers, and will also sell them, if desired, with a guarantee to talk, or exchange, but do not blame us if you have to exchange all your lifetime. Or again, a peddler will offer you a young bird resembling very much a Parrot, in size a little larger than a sparrow, claiming it to be just a very young genuine Mexican Parrot, while in fact it is only a Mexican Paroquet. Young Mexican Parrots, when they come on the market, are always as large as a common pigeon.

EDUCATED PARROTS
We always have a few already educated Parrots on hand, which average in price from $35.00 to $100.00, or more, according to kind and talking quality. Full particulars on application.

MAX GEISLER BIRD CO., OMAHA, NEB. AND NEW YORK CITY

MACCAWS AND COCKATOOS

Maccaws are the largest Parrots known, with extra long tail feathers and beautiful colored plumage, and usually become good talkers.

Cockatoos belong also to the parrot family. They differ by being provided with a "crest," either short or long, which they erect when excited.

Rose-breasted Cockatoo

Red and Blue Maccaw.............................$35.00 to $50.00
Blue Maccaw .... 35.00 to 50.00
Rose-breasted Cockatoo 18.00
Large Yellow-crested Cockatoo.............................. 30.00
Small Yellow-crested Cockatoo.............................. 20.00
Leadbeater Cockatoo 75.00
Red-crested Manilla Cockatoo.............................. 75.00

PAROQUETS AND LORIES

For shell Paroquets and Lovebirds medium sized brass canary cages are best.

Shell Paroquets With Young One.

Some learn to talk a little and are otherwise very intelligent, great pets and beautifully plumaged. Most all kinds will also breed easily in captivity. **Pair**

Australian Shell Paroquets
   (Lovebirds) ....$ 8.50
Yellow Shell Paroquets... 10.00
Blue Lovebirds (very rare) 15.00
Bee-Bee Paroquets........ 10.00
Yellow-faced Paroquets.... 10.00
Australian Cockatillos
   (nicely crested) 25.00
Blue Mountain Lories(most
   beautifully plumaged).. 35.00
Mexican Paroquets, each.. 4.50

MAX GEISLER BIRD CO., OMAHA, NEB. AND NEW YORK CITY

CANARIES

We are direct Importers of German Canaries—our European House being located in Hannover—Stromeyer St., Germany. We import in average about 100,000 Canaries every year, which we wholesale to other Bird Dealers except our special and registered strain of "Living Music Box." These birds are only obtainable direct from us as we do not sell these to other Dealers. This strain of Canaries are St. Andreasberg Roller Canaries, especially bred for us over in Germany and consists of the finest trained Rollers in existence. In order to protect ourselves and our patrons against imitators, we have registered in the patent office of the U. S. under the name of "Living Music Box," U. S. Patent No. 50853. This registered name will be stamped on the inside wing of each Roller and also on his shipping cage, and is a surety to you that you have received a genuine "Living Music Box."

The song of these birds is actually a stream of sweet music entirely different from the American canary and as it consists of trained notes, such as long, hollow rolls, trills, bell and nightingale notes, etc., which are produced with such a soft, melodious voice that it is really a pleasure to listen to such a little song wonder. While the sharp, shrill voice and short notes of the American Canary usually tires your ear, you will never get tired listening to the beautiful notes of "Living Music Box." These birds are also trained to sing at night as long as the room is light. For full particulars write for our testimonial sheet.

We Furnish a Written Guarantee with every Canary

Full and valuable directions how to feed and take proper care of Canaries will be found on the back of each package of our "Genuine Imported Roller Seed," and on page 60 of this catalog.

THE "LIVING MUSIC BOX"
U. S. Patent No. 50853

Guaranteed Singers ....$10.00   Female $3.50
Choice Selected Singers................ 12.00
Prize Singers or Trainers.............. 20.00 Upward

	Singer	Female
German Hartz Mountain Canaries.................	$ 6.00	$ 2.00
Choppers, the jazz singer of today, having both Roller and Hartz Mountain notes..	$ 8.00 to $10.00	2.50
White Canaries, very different, being white in place of yellow, having wonderful roller notes	$10.00 to $15.00	5.00

	Singer	Female
Yorkshire Canaries	$15.00	$ 6.00
Norwich Canaries	15.00	6.00
English Cayenne-red Canaries, the most beautiful Canaries in existence, their plumage being almost red...............	16.50	7.00
Manchester Coppies, the largest Canaries known with beautiful top-knots...........	Pair	40.00
Lizard Canaries, Golden or Silver Spangled..	Pair	40.00

What Some of Our Patrons Have to Say About Our "Living Music Box."

Mrs. R. H. Glenn, 2801 34th avenue, South, Seattle, Wash., writes: "Just a few lines, my birds arrived in first class shape, this morning. Wish I could express my thanks and appreciation in person for your wonderful selection. Am more than pleased in every way 'Billie' as I wish to call him, is the sweetest, most beautiful songster in the world. Have never heard one like him and would not take one hundred dollars for my lovly bird.

"Everyone that hears my birds, ask what kind of birds are these, never before heard any sing like yours. I enjoy telling people these are the famous 'Geisler Rollers' the World's Best."

Mrs. C. P. Jones, Battle Creek, Iowa, writes: "I feel it my duty to acknowledge the lovely little 'Living Music Box' canary as you call them. He wanted a bath at once after his box was opened and then he begun within an hour his little roll and is surely doing his duty. One could ask for nothing nicer. Don't be at all surprised if you receive duplicate orders of him."

Mrs. Alvah H. Burwick, 524 N. Liberty street, Webb City, Mo., writes: "I just must write again and tell you how much my two daughters, husband and I enjoy that wonderful singer (Happy) you sent us last May. I couldn't think of a more appropriate name for him, for he seems to sing and be happy at all times, cloudy days as well as shiny ones. I cover his cage of nights to keep him from singing too much, but that doesn't stop if we are in the same room with him he sings just the same until the light is turned off.

"I have never fed him any food besides yours and just like the directions call for on the Seed box. We couldn't tell he was moulting this fall only by his fallen feathers, for he never stopped singing at all. We just love him and he is not for sale at any price. A lot of my friends remark, 'Isn't that the finest singer you have ever heard and no one can surely be lonesome around him'."

Mrs. C. W. Boellstroff, Johnson, Nebr., writes: "I am more than pleased with the White Roller purchased from you. He seems perfection itself."

Frederick W. Smith, 7 Colonial street, Waterville, Maine, writes: "I cannot refrain from expressing my appreciation and satisfaction with the treatment I received from you, and also with the birds that I received this morning. The 'Living Music Box' was singing in the hands of the expressman as he delivered it to me at the door, and three of the other birds burst into song within fifteen minutes. I consider that remarkable.

I could have bought birds cheaper from other concerns, for I had price lists from them, but your willingness to make me satisfied with my purchases from you led me to believe that I should be more satisfied with the birds that I purchased from you than those from other dealers. It was not the price that led me to make my purchase from you as much as your courtesy and your fairness. So I thank you again."

MAX GEISLER BIRD CO., OMAHA, NEB. AND NEW YORK CITY

CHOICE SONGSTERS

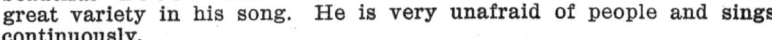

Under this class we give a variety of the **best singing** birds kept in captivity, and espec-ially recommend the following, which we have always found to give good satisfaction, and which we usually keep in stock all the year around.

The well k n o w n **Shama Thrush** imported from India is also called the "King of Song" on account of his most beautiful n o t e s and

Shama Thrush

great variety in his song. He is very unafraid of people and **sings** continuously.

The **"Chinese or Pekin Nightingale,"** a most beautiful plumaged, very active bird of the size of a canary and an excellent, fine **singer,** which his name already indicates. This bird always gives best satis-faction to everyone and cannot be highly enough recommended.

"Brazilian or Gray Cardinal." These birds bring in their song some very **fine notes, something similar to a** Nightingale. We always keep a good stock of this kind on hand, and there-fore we are able to select some extra fine songsters.

For Suitable Cages See Nos. 248 to 252

	Warranted Males
Shama Thrush	$25.00
Shama Thrush, extra fine selected songsters.......	$30.00-35.00
Brazilian Gray Cardinals..	7.50
Brazilian Gray Cardinals, selected singers	10.00
Chinese or Pekin Night-ingales	8.50
Chinese or Pekin Nightin-gales, extra fine selected songsters	10.00

Brazilian Gray Cardinal

Rev. Accursius, Hays, Kansas, writes: "I am pleased to inform you of the arrival of my Gold Finch, he is a beautiful singer."

Dr. E. J. Kauffman, Marion, So. Dak., writes: "'The Shama Thrush' that we received from you a month or so ago, cannot be over estimated. He is a beautiful singer and if there is anything that spreads sunshine in a home, it is a bird of this kind. We are certainly more than pleased with him."

Mrs. Leo. Bierman, Route 3, Norfolk, Nebr., writes: The Straw-berry Finches I got from you sometime ago are beautiful, they surely have a beautiful song.

MAX GEISLER BIRD CO., OMAHA, NEB. AND NEW YORK CITY

European Robin

Chinese Nightingale

Warranted Males

European Nightingales....$25.00

European Blackcap, or
Blackheaded Nightingale 20.00

European Goldfinches..... 5.00

Europan Linnets 4.50

European Siskins........ 3.50

Russian Goldfinch

European Bullfinch

European Chaffinches 3.50

European Bullfinches 8.00

Females $4.00

European Bullfinches, trained to whistle 1 to 3 tunes...... 30.00-50.00

South American Troopials (like Mocking Bird)........... 12.00

East India Minor, can be taught to talk................... 25.00

J. H. Daniel, Gonzales, Texas, writes: "'The Living Music Box' reached me in good shape and am well pleased. I told you the White Canary was going to the Fair, it did and got a Blue Ribbon, it sure attracted a lot of attention."

MAX GEISLER BIRD CO., OMAHA, NEB. AND NEW YORK CITY

OTHER SINGING AND FANCY BIRDS

A collection of very handsome birds, mostly very small
in size. They are easy to be
taken care of and are very
hardy. Most all will breed
with good success, especially
if kept in an aviary.

An aviary filled with a few
pairs of the smallest, bright-
colored red-billed Finches is
the nicest attraction one can
think of.

Australian Zebra Finches and
Young One

For suitable cages see Nos. 219-220-220a

	Pair
Australian Zebra Finches, small beautiful birds, with bright red bills; breed easy in captivity	$10.00
Society Finches, small birds which breed freely in a cage	8.00
Strawberry Finches, one of the smallest birds kept in captivity, beautiful bright red plumage, with small white dots, red bill, very sweet singers	8.00
Cordon Blue Finches, same size as foregoing, beautiful blue plumage, red cheeks, red bill	8.00

Orange Cheek   Orange Breast   Cordon Blue
Waxbill   Strawberry

	Pair
Waxbill, same size as foregoing, nice brown plumage, red bill and red stripe on each side of head	$ 7.50
Orange Cheek Finches, same size as foregoing, with orange spots on both sides of head	7.50

Pair

Negro Finches, same size as foregoing, jet black plumage......$ 9.00

Black-headed Nuns, a little larger than foregoing, brown with
  black heads, very cute.................................... 9.00

White-headed Nuns, same as foregoing, but with white head.... 9.00

Three-colored Nuns, same as foregoing; but the lower side of the
  body is white... 9.00

Cut-throat Finches, about one-half the size of a Canary, plumage brown except the throat, which is white with a red stripe
  through the center.. 7.50

White Java Canaries or Rice Birds,
size of common Canary, pure white
with pink bill; very beautiful, and
also very sweet singers and easy
breeders. We can highly recommend them........................ 16.00

Single Males, warranted singers...... 10.00

Single Females 7.00

Gray Java Rice Birds same as foregoing, but plumage of a bluish gray

White Java Canary   color, with white cheeks........... 7.00

Napoleon Weavers, orange yellow with brown wings, black
  throat; this and the following kind are especially admired
  for their wonderful ability in building odd-shaped hanging
  nests 10.00

Common Weavers, reddish-brown, black cheeks and throat, red
  bill 8.00

Paradise Finches, beautiful birds, with long, drooping tail-feath-
  ers, which measure about three times the length of the whole
  body, plumage black, goldish-brown neck and breast, lower
  part of the body pure white............................... 15.00

Lady Gould's Finches, in most brilliant colors, pair............. 25.00

Pintail Nonpareils, in most brilliant colors, pair.............. 12.00

FERRETS

Ferrets are natural enemies of rats and will drive out all rats.
They are generally of a good disposition and readily become pets. If
you are troubled with rats buy a pair of ferrets and they will soon
clean your entire premises.

Write For Prices

FOR YOUR ESTATE OR PARK

FANCY FOWLS

We import direct from India and other foreign countries, "Fancy Fowls" such as Burmese Peacocks, Jungle Fowl; Peacock, Fire-Back, Kalitz, Monal Pheasants; Chucar, Partridges; Wild Ducks; Tabiru, Adjutant, Storks; Sarus, Demoiselle, Cranes; Flamingos; White and Black Swans, etc.

If interested, write for prices to our New York House.

Golden Pheasant

PETS AND RARE ANIMALS

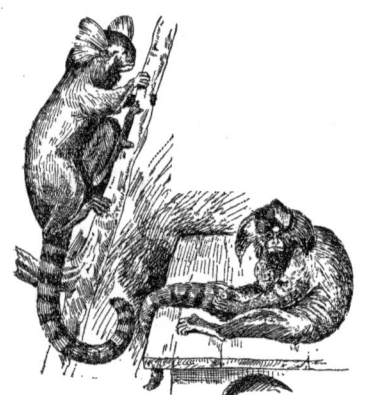

Marmozette Monkeys

Rhesus Monkey

	Each
Rhesus Monkeys	$25.00 Up
Java Monkeys	20.00 Up
Ringtail Monkeys	25.00 Up
Marmozette Monkeys (the smallest monkey in existence)	25.00
Per Pair	45.00
European Red Squirrels	5.00
Common Rabbits	2.00
Guinea Pigs	1.25

MAX GEISLER BIRD CO., OMAHA, NEB. AND NEW YORK CITY

ANGORA KITTEN

The largest and most beautiful among all Cats, almost double
the size of an ordinary cat. They have big bright eyes and
very long, silky hair (from two to three inches when full
grown), especially long on the chest and sides of the head,
thus giving them an odd appearance, which makes the An-
goras so admirable; they are great pets and excellent
ratters ....$8.00 to $10.00

Maltese Kitten 3.00

JAPANESE DANCING MICE

Wonderful window attraction as they are always dancing—nice
novelty for children.

Pair

Japanese Dancing Mice...$3.50

White Mice 1.00

White Rats 1.00

Chameleons, the latest pets, perfectly harmless; they are specially noted for their ability of changing colors; only in
season during the summer months, each.................. .50

MAX GEISLER BIRD CO., OMAHA, NEB. AND NEW YORK CITY

DOGS

We handle nothing but **thoroughbred** Dogs. Breeds which are not mentioned in this catalogue will be furnished at short notice. Prices below are for puppies.

Poodle

Fox Terrier

	Average Price For A Good Dog, Each
White Silk or Maltese Poodles	$15.00
Wire Hair Fox Terriers	40.00
Fox Terriers	10.00
White Spitz	12.00
Cocker Spaniels	25.00
German Police Dogs	15.00
Bull Terrier	20.00
Boston Terrier	25.00
Scotch Collies	12.00
Hunting Dogs	15.00

Boston Terrier

Russian Wolfhound and
St. Bernard

MAX GEISLER BIRD CO., OMAHA, NEB. AND NEW YORK CITY

FANCY FISH

| Japanese Fantail | German Goldfish | Japanese Comet |
| Japanese Fringetail | | Chinese Telescope |

Our specialties are Japanese and Chinese Goldfish, of which we only handle the **genuine imported** stock, short, egg-shaped body, good fins and tail, and brilliant colors. We ship fish with perfect safety by express, in properly fitted cans which we charge for from 25 cents to 50c, according to size. When ordering Fish would advise you send 40 cents extra for a box of Daphina Fish Food and a bunch of Aquatic Plants. The first has printed directions on the care of Goldfish and the aquarium, the latter will save you the trouble of changing the water so often (read article on following page), and besides will beautify your aquarium very much, especially if the plants are attached to one of the nice aquarium ornaments offered on pages 22 to 24.

	Each
Japanese Fantail Goldfish, according to size	$0.50 to $1.25
Japanese Fringetail Goldfish, according to size	.75 to 1.50
Japanese Comet Goldfish, according to size	.25 to .50
Chinese Telescope Goldfish, pure black, according to size	.75 to 1.50
German Goldfish, according to size	.10 to .50
Small Turtles	.25
Tadpoles	.10
Small Snails	.05
Large Snails	.15

Prices of large two-year-old Breeders of Japanese Fantails, Fringetails, Telescopes and German Goldfish on application.

BREED FISH

The newest fad is to breed tropical fish in a 2 gallon bowl. Much easier to take care of as they require warmer water and therefore need little changing. Paradise must be kept alone.

Pair

Paradise Fish, beautiful striped fish; will spawn in the bowl....$2.00

Zebra Fish (egg bearing)...................................... 2.00

Sword Tails (life bearing)..................................... 2.25

Gouppi (life bearing)... .75

AQUATIC PLANTS

It is impossible to keep Goldfish in good health any length of time without Aquatic P l a n t s. Why? Simply because the fish absorb oxygen when breathing and when kept in an aquarium where no aquatic plants are grown they will soon have consumed all the oxygen contained in the water, and then they are forced to come to the surface in order to get

Potamogaton and Cabomba

oxygen out of the air. But as fish are not built to breathe through the air, their gills will soon become inflamed, thus causing the death of the fish. While on the other hand, Aquatic Plants by growing give oxygen to the water, thus supplying the fish with this life-giving element all the time. Of course the water could be changed frequently, which you would have to do, if you should not keep any Aquatic Plants, but to say nothing about all the trouble and inconvenience of changing water every day, Goldfish are naturally used to standing water, and therefore the constant changing will do them harm and you will never be able to keep Goldfish with good success.

Prepaid by Mail.

Cabomba Palustris (like picture), bright green when in season ....25c bunch

Myriaphylum Spicatum (Water Milfoil) very handsome.....25c bunch

Water Hyacinthas, grows floating on surface of water.......25c each

The following three kinds grow better if imbedded in soil or sand.

Vallisneria Spiralis, a grass-like plant, very effective........35c bunch

Potomogaton (like picture) very handsome plant..........,.35c bunch

Ludwigia Mullerti, grows rather bushy, bright green, and redish-green, very handsome........................35c bunch

MAX GEISLER BIRD CO., OMAHA, NEB. AND NEW YORK CITY

FISH GLOBES

Style A   **Style B**   **Style C**

		Each
Style A	1 gallon Clear	$0.65
	1 gallon Green	.85
	2 gallon Clear	1.10
	2 gallon Green	1.50
Style B	1 gallon Clear	.65
	1 gallon Green	.85
	2 gallon Clear	1.10
	2 gallon Green	1.50
Style C	1 gallon Clear	.65
	1 gallon Green	.85
	2 gallon Clear	1.10
	2 gallon Green	1.50

Round Globes (Clear)   **Globe on Separate Foot**

3 Gallon Capacity........$1.75   3 Gallon Capacity........$2.00

4 Gallon Capacity......... 2.00   4 Gallon Capacity........ 2.25

MAX GEISLER BIRD CO., OMAHA, NEB. AND NEW YORK CITY

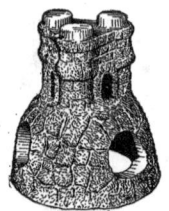

| 1 and 2 | 3 and 4 | 5 and 6 |

	Each		Each
	Each		Each
No. 1—2½ inches	$0.15	Prepaid....	$0.25
No. 2—3½ inches	.30	Prepaid....	.40
No. 3—2½ inches	.15	Prepaid....	.25
No. 4—3½ inches	.30	Prepaid....	.40
No. 5—5 inches	.40	Prepaid....	.55
No. 6—6 inches	.50	Prepaid....	.70

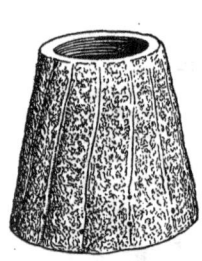

| 7 | 8 and 9 | 10 | 11 |

	Each		Each
No. 7—4 inches	$0.20	Prepaid....	$0.30
No. 8—4½ inches	.45	Prepaid....	.60
No. 9—6½ inches	.75	Prepaid....	.95
No. 10—5½ inches	.45	Prepaid....	.60
No. 11—5½ inches	.45	Prepaid....	.60

NEW COLORED ORNAMENTS

The latest in ornaments, highly colored in green, red, blue and yellow shaded together.

  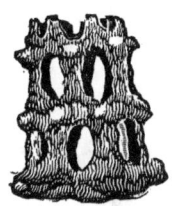

| 12 and 13 | 14 | 15 |

			Each		Each
No. 12—4½	inches	....	$0.40	Prepaid....	$0.55
No. 13—6	inches	....	.60	Prepaid....	.80
No. 14—5	inches	....	.60	Prepaid....	.75
No. 15—3½	inches	....	.35	Prepaid....	.50

  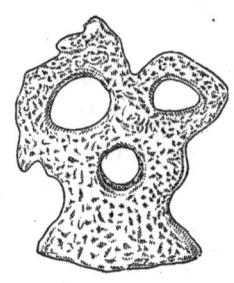

| 16 | 17 | 18 and 18 |

			Each		Each
No. 16—4½	inches	....	$0.45	Prepaid....	$0.60
No. 17—5	inches	....	.40	Prepaid....	.55
No. 18—4	inches	....	.35	Prepaid....	.50
No. 19—5	inches	....	.45	Prepaid....	.60

POPULAR COLORED AQUARIUM NOVELTIES

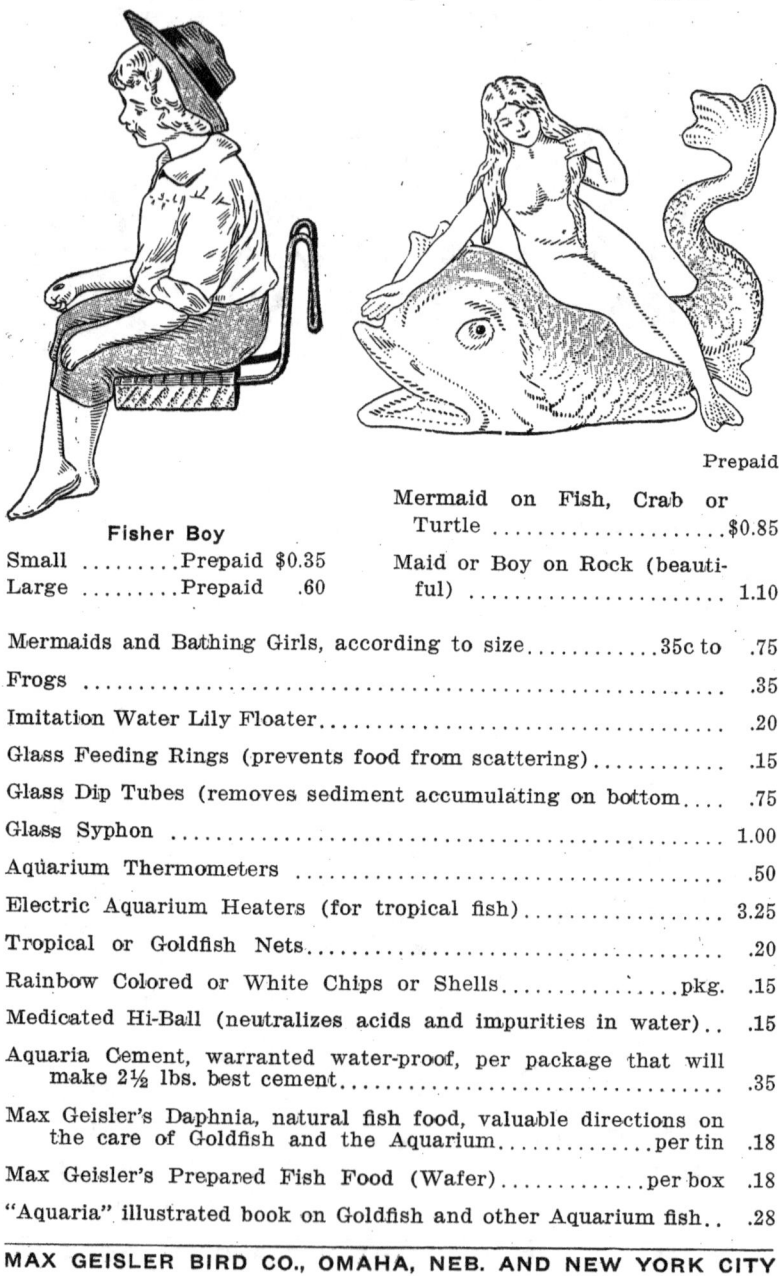

Prepaid

Fisher Boy

Small ....Prepaid $0.35

Large ....Prepaid .60

Mermaid on Fish, Crab or Turtle $0.85

Maid or Boy on Rock (beautiful) 1.10

Mermaids and Bathing Girls, according to size...........35c to .75

Frogs .... .35

Imitation Water Lily Floater.................................... .20

Glass Feeding Rings (prevents food from scattering)........... .15

Glass Dip Tubes (removes sediment accumulating on bottom.... .75

Glass Syphon 1.00

Aquarium Thermometers .... .50

Electric Aquarium Heaters (for tropical fish)................. 3.25

Tropical or Goldfish Nets..................................... .20

Rainbow Colored or White Chips or Shells...............pkg. .15

Medicated Hi-Ball (neutralizes acids and impurities in water).. .15

Aquaria Cement, warranted water-proof, per package that will make 2½ lbs. best cement.................................. .35

Max Geisler's Daphnia, natural fish food, valuable directions on the care of Goldfish and the Aquarium.............per tin .18

Max Geisler's Prepared Fish Food (Wafer)............per box .18

"Aquaria" illustrated book on Goldfish and other Aquarium fish.. .28

ALUMINUM FRAME AQUARIUMS

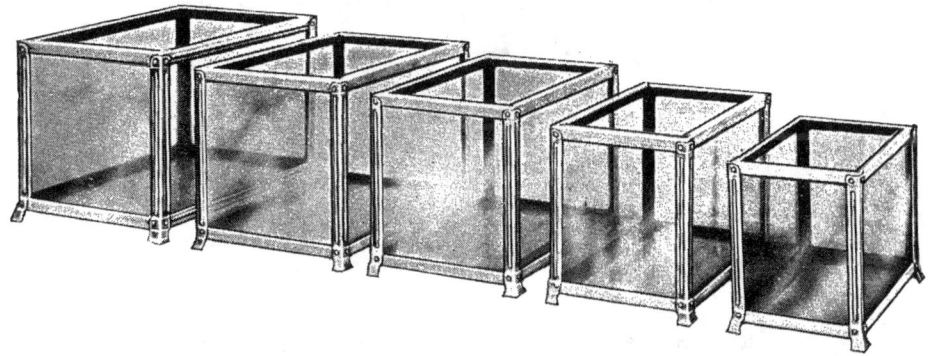

The Aluminum Frame Aquariums shown here are of heavy gauge aluminum, properly formed and ribbed to insure the greatest possible strength. Being rustproof, they are easily kept sanitary and highly polished.

Top and bottom sections of frame are one piece, resulting in a very substantial construction. These, and the standards with feet formed in one piece, are securely riveted.

These Aquariums are glazed with double strength glass; the bottoms of heavy glass. Made in the following sizes only:

No.	Lgth.	Width	Hght.	Capac.	Wght.	Price
03	12½″	8½″	8⅝″	3 gal.	5¼ lbs.	$ 5.50
04	13½″	9½″	9¼″	4 gal.	7 lbs.	6.50
11	16¾″	8½″	10¾″	5 gal.	10 lbs.	11.00
12	18⅜″	10½″	10¾″	7 gal.	11½ lbs.	13.50

STEEL FRAME AQUARIUMS

The Steel Frame Aquariums are of the same general construction as the Aluminum Frame previously described, but using steel of the proper strength in place of aluminum. Attractively finished in dark green. Same sizes as above:

No. 03 Steel $5.00
No. 04 Steel 6.00

No.	Lgth.	Width	Hght.	Capac.	Wght.	Price
61	20″	10″	10″	5 gal.	25 lbs.	$12.50
63	24″	12″	12″	12 gal.	33 lbs.	15.00
64	30″	12″	12″	15 gal.	45 lbs.	20.00

SHEET IRON AQUARIUM WITH GLASS BOTTOMS

The steel frames are finished in green color. **The bottoms are of heavy glass.**

No.	Lgth.	Width	Hght.	About	Wght.	Price
101	10″	6″	7″	1.5 gal.	6 lbs.	$ 2.00
102	12″	7″	7″	2.0 gal.	7 lbs.	4.00
103	14″	8″	10″	4.8 gal.	11 lbs.	5.00
104	16″	9½″	10″	6.0 gal.	13 lbs.	6.00
106	18¾″	11⅛″	12″	10.0 gal.	22 lbs.	12.00

All White Glass Aquariums

Made of one piece heavy glass with smooth rolled edges.

3 Gallon Capacity.......................................$3.75 Each

ARTISTIC AQUARIA

 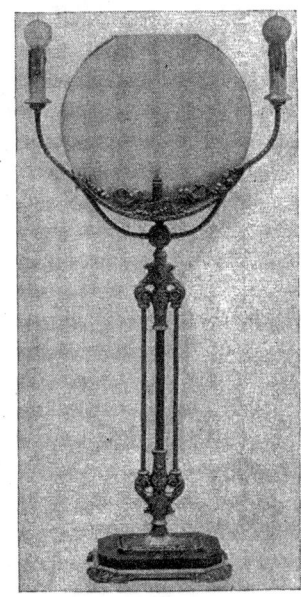

1970
Height, 42 inch
$15.00 Complete

1971
Height, 42 inch
$20.00 Complete

Both Nos. 1970 and 1971 are finished in antique gold. Bowl of green colored glass. No. 1971 is wired for electricity, showing the fish to their full advantage.

A magnificent addition to any home.

A THING OF BEAUTY AND UTILITY

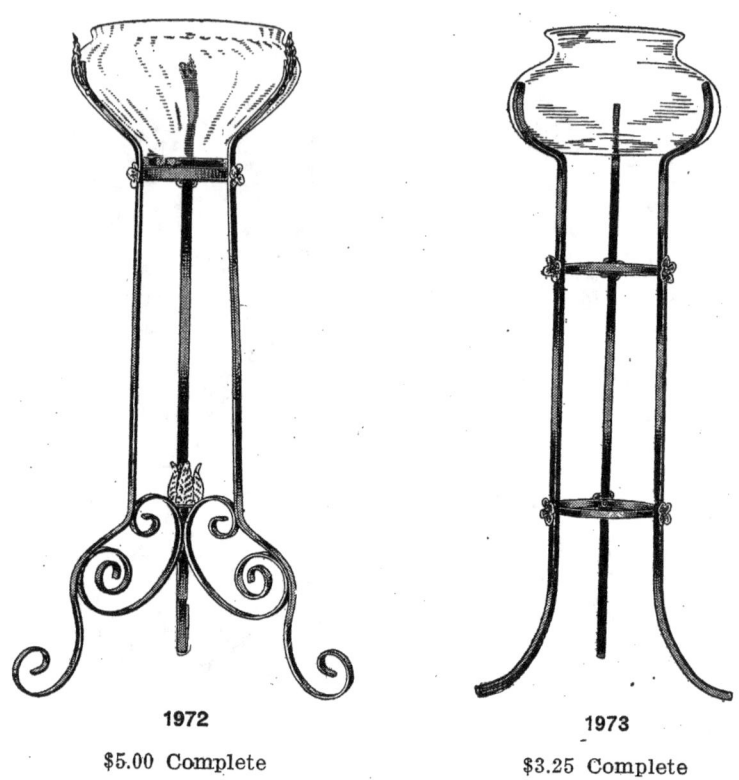

1972   **1973**

$5.00 Complete $3.25 Complete

No. 1972—Dark green wrought iron, with decorations. Bowl 2 gal. green glass, as style C on page 21.

No. 1973—With 2 gal. clear glass bowl as style A on page 21.

No. 1974—Wrought iron stand similar to No. 1973, with 2 gal. clear bowl as style B on page 21—$3.25.

MAX GEISLER BIRD CO., OMAHA, NEB. AND NEW YORK CITY

CAGES

We make a specialty of Hendryx and Leon cages, which have a reputation all over the United States as the most stylish and best finished Bird Cages manufactured. The material used is of high-grade quality; no poisonous oxides, or other matter injurious to birds enter into the construction of these Cages. The cross-bars of all Cages are one solid piece of metal, which makes the Cage very durable and prevents it from losing its original shape. After being finished they are provided with a coat of very hard metal lacquer, which avoids all tarnishing.

No. 199

No. 199—With drawer bottom 10¾ in. diam. Ivory, Red, Blue and Green with contrasting color $8.00

No. 214

No. 215

No. 214, Brass...........$12.00
   8¾x8¾x15½ height.

No. 215, Brass............$3.40
   10 inch diameter.

No. 216, Brass............$2.60
   10⅛ inch diameter.

No. 216a, Brass...........$3.00
   11 inch diameter.

No. 216b, Brass...........$3.20
   11¾ inch diameter.

No. 217, Red with black
   trim $10.50
   12½ inch diameter.

No. 216
No. 126a
No. 216b

No. 217

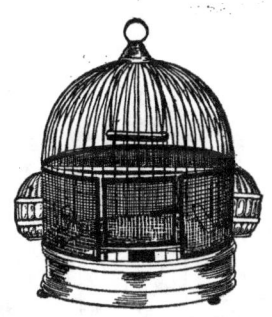

No. 210 ....$3.00
10 inch diameter.
Red, blue or green.

No. 211, Brass............$4.15
10 inch diameter.

No. 211a $4.50
10¾ inch diameter.

No. 211b $5.00
11½ inch diameter.

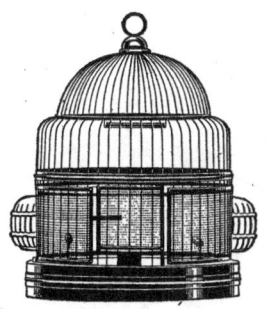

No. 212 ....$5.75
10¾ inch diameter.
Gun Metal and Brass Trim.

No. 212a $5.75
Dull Brass with Polish Brass
Trimming.

No. 213, Brass............$2.60
10 inch diameter.

No. 213a $3.00
11 inch Diameter.

No. 213b $3.25
12 inch diameter.

CLOSE WIRE BRASS CAGES
Suitable for Strawberry Finches and other small birds.

No. 219—$8.00

All Brass, Close Wire

9½x6½x12½ Height

No. 19a $10.00

11½x8x13½

All Enameled Close Wire

No. 220...................$3.75

Size 8⅝x5⅝, height 11⅝ in.

No. 220a $5.00

10½x7x13½ in. height.

GLASS SIDED CANARY CAGES

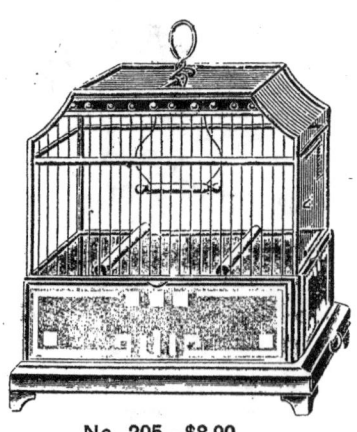

No. 205—$8.00

All Brass

No. 206—$10.00

All Brass

MAX GEISLER BIRD CO., OMAHA, NEB. AND NEW YORK CITY

Diameter, 10 in.

Height, 17⅝ in

No. 207, Brass............$7.75

No. 207a, Duco $7.75

Duco in following colors: Chinese red and black, ivory and red trim, green and coral.

No. 207

All Brass

No. 208, with Fender.....$11.00
Body 12 inches in diameter,
Height, 15½ inches

No. 209, with Fender.....$15.00
Body 15 inches in diameter,
Height, 19 inches.

All Brass

No. 209, dull brass........$12.00

No. 209, with Fender..........

No. 209a, Polished Brass or Antique Copper, with Fender....

Size, 8¾x8¾ inches,
Height 15¼ inches.

PYRALIN

The Very Latest in Bird Cages, Manufactured Only By "Hendryx"

New principles in decorative values and design are presented in "Hendryx" Bird Cages and Stands made entirely of "Pyralin."

Made from solid "Pyralin" in Black, White, or colors, they offer a rich lustrous finish, with permanence of color as well as durability.

The attractive designs and the variety of color combinations allow selection to harmonize with other interior settings of the home.

They are strongly constructed, yet may be easily taken apart and cleaned in a few minutes with a damp cloth, or with soap and warm water.

The use of "Pyralin" and the design and construction of these cages and stands mark a decided advance in the principles of manufacture.

No. 221   No. 222

$13.50 $20.00

For Colors See Page Opposite

PYRALIN OUTFITS

Cages or Outfits Come in the Following Colors

Red and Black
Green and Black
Green and White
Black and White

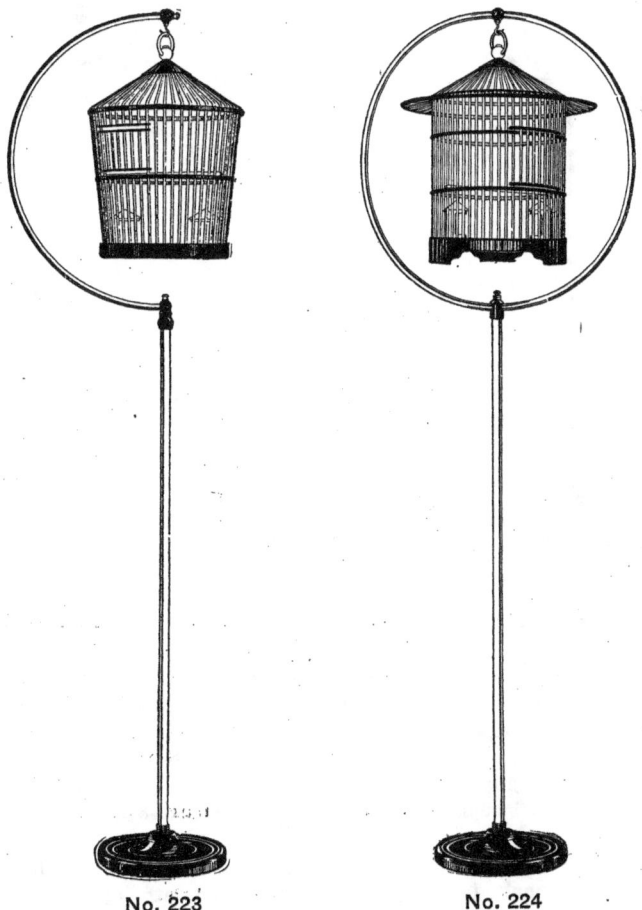

No. 223   No. 224

No. 223—$22.50   No. 224—$32.00

MAX GEISLER BIRD CO., OMAHA, NEB. AND NEW YORK CITY

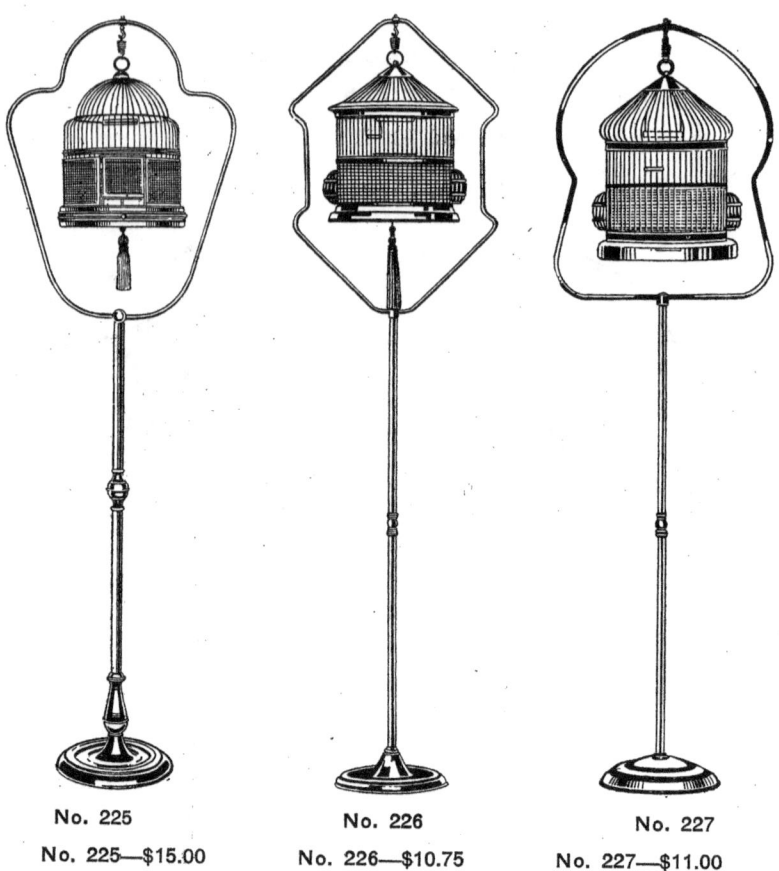

No. 225   No. 226   No. 227

No. 225—$15.00   No. 226—$10.75   No. 227—$11.00

No. 225—Modernistic finish, drawer bottom cage, solid brass showing thru the color. Colors: Red on brass, green on brass, blue on brass, black on brass.

No. 226—Highly attractive two-tone finishes. Colors: Orchid and brass, blue and brass, red and brass, green and brass.

No. 227—Good looking, shaded effects. Colors: Red shaded into lighter, green shaded into lighter, blue shaded into lighter.

These must be seen to be appreciated.

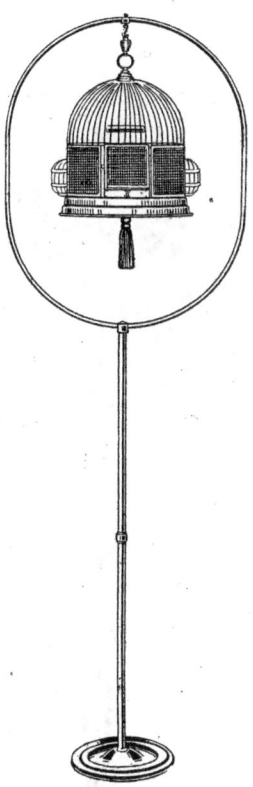 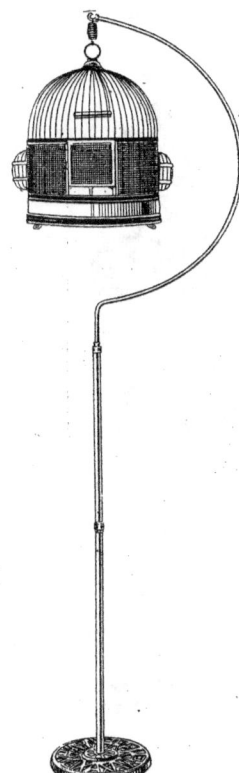

No. 228—$5.25

Two-Tone finish.

Colors: Red, blue, green or all brass.

No. 228A—$2.50
Stand Only

No. 229—$5.00

Colors: Red, blue, green or all brass.

For an inexpensive outfit this cannot be beat.

No. 229a—$2.40
Stand Only

VERY DIFFERENT AND VERY ATTRACTIVE

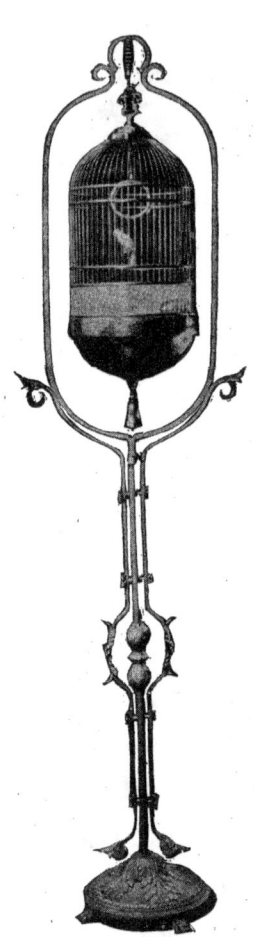

No. 230—$35.00

Ivory and Brown

No. 231—$25.00

Green

PARROT STANDS

No. 232—$16.50

All Brass with spun aluminum
cups, heavy base

No. 233—$11.50
All Brass
No. 233a—Bronze finish....$7.50

These above have black japanned tray.

Just the Thing for Polly

For Stand Cover See Page 41

PARROT CAGES

Steel Wire

No. 234 . . . .$11.00
  Size 13¼x15 in., height
  22 in.

No. 235 . . . .$12.50
  Size 15x17½ in., height
  24 in.

All Brass

No. 236 . . . .$20.00
  Size 13x15 in., height
  20 in.

No. 237 . . . .$22.50
  Size 15x17½ in., height
  22½ in.

**Square Parrot Cage With
Drawer Base**

ROUND PARROT CAGES

Tinned Wire

No. 238 . . . .$5.25
  Size 13 in. in diam-
  eter, height 19½ in.

No. 239 . . . .$6.50
  Size 14½ in. in di-
  ameter, height 22 in.

No. 240 . . . .$8.00
  Size 16 in. in diam-
  eter, height 23½ in.

No. 241 . . . .$15.00
  All Solid Brass
  Size 16 in. in diam-
  eter, height 22½ in.

COLLAPSIBLE
PARROT
CAGE

Made of Tinned Steel
With Tin Drawer Base

No. 242—$6.75

12 in. x 14½ in. x 15½
in. height

No. 243

PARROT STAND COVER

All Brass

Will fit Parrot stands 233 and
233a Listed on Page 39.

Brass $11.00
Steel 7.50

MAX GEISLER BIRD CO., OMAHA, NEB. AND NEW YORK CITY

BREEDING CAGES
Enameled.

	Each
No. 244, double, size 18x10 in. x 12 in. high	$5.50
No. 245, double, size 20x11 in. x 13 in. high	6.25
No. 247, double, size 22x12 in. x 14 in. high	7.50

Drawers in these cages.

FOR REDBIRD, MOCKINGBIRD, ETC.

Durable "all metal" Cages, enameled, vermin proof.

No. 248, size 10x16 in., height 14½ in. $5.50

No. 250, size 12x 20¼ in., height 18 in. $6.50

No. 252, size 14¼x 24 in., height 21½ in. $8.00

Drawer in these cages.

MAX GEISLER BIRD CO., OMAHA, NEB. AND NEW YORK CITY

Enameled

No. 253 ....$2.00
Size 9¾x6½ in.,
height, 12⅝ in.

No. 254 ....$2.50
Size 11x7½ in.,
height 14 in.

**Canary
Traveling
Cage**

Enameled Vermin
Proof.

No. 256, with
drawer $1.45

All Brass

No. 257 ....$3.00
Size 9½x6⅜ in.,
height 12½ in.

No. 259 ....$3.75
Size 10¾x7¾ in.
height 13 in.

No. 260 ....$4.50
Size 13x8¼ in.,
height 14½ in.

BRASS GUARD CLOTH, WITH CLASPS

These prevent the bird from scattering seed or gravel on the floor, and are at the same time a very handsome ornament to the cage. When ordering, give number of cage or the exact length and width of same, and name of manufacturer.

4 inches wide—per foot.........................35c Prepaid....40c

BRACKETS

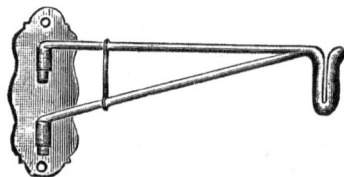

Swinging Bracket, Brass or White Enamel.

The only means by which to hang a cage to the wall.

Each
Each ......15c Prepaid....20c

SCREW BRACKETS

Extra heavy, for Parrot cages, 12 in. long

Japanned ....25c Prepaid....30c

BRASS SPRINGS

Each   Each

Brass or colored springs................10c Prepaid....15c

Extra large, heavy brass spring for Parrot, Redbird Cages, etc................25c Prepaid....30c

Brass Spring

Perch Scrapers

	Each		Each
For Canary Cages........	15c	Prepaid....	20c

PARROT PERCHES

	Each		Each
Plain	20c	Prepaid....	25c

CANARY PERCHES

	Each		Each
Round Wood Perches.....	10c	Prepaid....	13c

When ordering give size of cage from wire to wire.

Canary Swings, brass.....	15c	Prepaid....	20c
Parrot Swings, tinned wire, plain	25c	Prepaid....	35c
Parrot Swings, brass wire fancy	45c	Prepaid....	55c
Parrot Foot Chains.......	75c	Prepaid....	80c

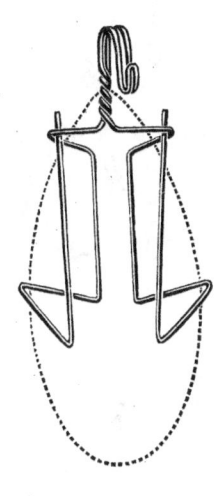

Cuttlefish Bone
Holders..each 10c

Prepaid 13c

With Bone, each 15c
3 for.......... 40c

Prepaid 18c

Prepared Bird Insect Powder and gun,
prepaid 35c
A sure death to lice or other vermin on Birds.

	Each		Each
Willow nests	10c	Prepaid....	15c
Wire nests	15c	Prepaid....	20c

	Each	Ppd.
Bird Nesting	10c	13c
6 for	50c	60c

By using this Nesting the young ones will not get any vermin.

MAX GEISLER BIRD CO., OMAHA, NEB. AND NEW YORK CITY

BRASS DOUBLE CAGE SPRING

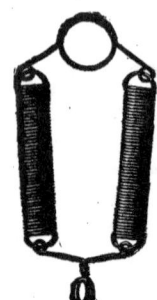

Will prevent Cage from swinging around. Very pretty, strong and elastic. The only perfect Cage Spring on the market.

Each ....Prepaid 25c

Adjustable Brass Ladder Chain
With Single Spring.

2 feet long............Prepaid, each 25c
3 feet long............Prepaid, each 35c

With Double Spring

2 feet long............Prepaid, each 40c
3 feet long............Prepaid, each 50c

OUTSIDE CANARY BATH

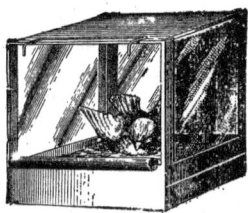

Style 1

85c prepaid

All white.

Style 2

$1.00 prepaid

Colored or brass duco.

These bath houses are to be used on the OUTSIDE of cage in front of open door and will fit all cages. It prevents the bird from splashing water all over the cage and room, and is the only means by which a bird can get a thorough bath. It is made of Jaapnned tin and has transparent celluloid lights.

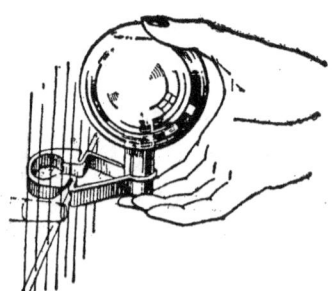

SOMETHING NEW

Crystal Fountain

Will keep water fresh for a week..each 75c Prepaid..85c

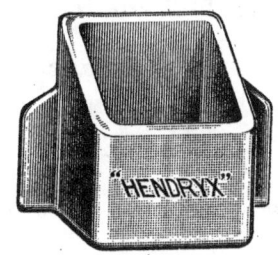

No. 1913.....20c   Prepaid..30c

No. 1913. Breeding cup
   Each ....25c Prepaid....35c

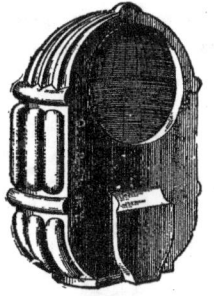

**Shell
Cups**

Each.....15c   Prepaid.....20c

Pyralin shell cups (unbreak-
able) ..each 20c Prepaid 25c

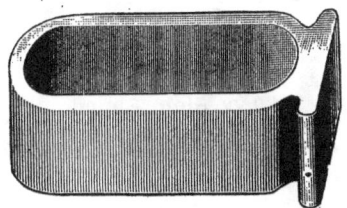

Treat or Food Holder

Actual size...........prepaid 10c

Porcelain Bathing Dishes

	Each		Each
Small size	15c	Prepaid....	25c
Medium size	20c	Prepaid....	30c
Parrot Cups of different styles...........	40c-60c	Prepaid..	50c-70c
Parrot Cups, for parrot stands..............	75c	Prepaid....	85c

DOG CHAINS

25c—50c—75c—$1.00
According to Weight.

LEATHER LEADS

Plain ....40c—60c—80c
French Snaps..75c—$1.00—$1.25
According to Width.

No. 1529

POLICE AND COLLIE COLLAR
Brass Stud Round
Russet or Black
17-19-21 in. long, each.....$3.00

No. 1524

Heavy Plain Round
Large Dogs $1.50
Small Dogs 1.00

No. 307

	F. L.	L. L.
12 to 16 in. long—½ in. wide	50c	$1.00
14 to 18 in. long—¾ in. wide		1.75

No. 312

	L. L.
9 to 13 in. long—⅜ in. wide	$1.00
14 to 18 in. long—¾ in. wide	1.50
17 to 24 in. long— 1 in. wide	2.00

No. 317

	F. L.	L. L.
12 to 16 in. long—⅝ in. wide		$1.25
17 to 24 in. long— 1 in. wide	$1.00	2.00

Initials F. L. means felt lined.
Initials L. L. mean leather lined.
Flat collars come in green, red, russet and black.

CHAIN CHOKE COLLARS
$1.00 each

MAX GEISLER BIRD CO., OMAHA, NEB. AND NEW YORK CITY

No. 205

LEATHER MUZZLE

Bulldog Shape 75c
Pet Dog Shape 75c
Collie Shape 75c

No. 230

HUMANE MUZZLE

All Breeds........$1.00 to $1.50

No. 3002

ROUND STUDS

Black, Russet
All Leather Lined

15-17-19 in. long, ½ in.
   wide $2.50
20-22-24 in. long, ⅝ in.
   wide 3.00
26-28-30 in. long, 1 in.
   wide 4.00

No. 2240

FELT LINED

Round or Diamond Studs
Red, Green, Black, Russet

15-17-19 in. long, ½ in.
   wide $1.00
20-22-24 in. long, ⅝ in.
   wide 1.25
22-24 in. long, ¾ in.
   wide 1.50

DOG BLANKETS
DOG SWEATERS

All Wool—Good Plaid

Size 10 to 14..............$2.00
Size 16 to 20.............. 2.50

DOG GRIPS

Made of Fibre
Also Dog Sleeping Baskets
(wicker).

Length
14 inch $3.50
16 inch 4.50
18 inch 5.00
20 inch 5.50

Catnip Balls or Mice, a beautiful and amusing toy for cats......15c, prepaid 17c

Catnip in packages, loose catnip and other herbs beneficial to cats..........15c, prepaid 17c

THE NEW TOY

For children as well as for dogs and cats—made of firm rubber — will "Me-ow" whenever pressed.

Large size........Prepaid $1.00

Small size........Prepaid .60

Rubber bones.....Prepaid .40

TAXIDERMY IN ALL ITS BRANCHES

Birds and Animals Mounted by Expert Taxidermists

Write For Prices For Mounting.

MAX GEISLER BIRD CO., OMAHA, NEB. AND NEW YORK CITY

DOG FOOD

**"Milk Bone" and
Ken-L-Ration**

These celebrated foods are supplied to all the leading kennels, and are used at the principal Dog Shows all over the world.

BENNETT'S "MILK BONE"

		Each		Each
Puppy Food	10 oz.	20c	Prepaid	30c
Puppy Food	26 oz.	40c	Prepaid	55c
Dog Food	11 oz.	20c	Prepaid	30c
Dog Food	29 oz.	40c	Prepaid	55c
Junior (small)	22 oz.	40c	Prepaid	55c
Cat Crumbs	11 oz.	20c	Prepaid	30c

Chappels Bros.' Canned Dog Food

Ken-L-Ration	per can 15c	Prepaid	25c
Kit-E-Ration	per can 15c	Prepaid	25c
Pup-E-Ration	per can 15c	Prepaid	25c
Hemo-Ration	per can 15c	Prepaid	25c
48-can case		not prepaid	$6.50

BULK DOG FOOD

Dog Biscuit	per pound 15c	Prepaid	25c
Puppy Biscuit	per pound 15c	Prepaid	25c
Kibbled Biscuit	per pound 15c	Prepaid	25c
Puppy Meal	per pound 15c	Prepaid	25c
100 pounds of above		not prepaid	$9.50

DOG MEDICINE

Delcreo—Tonic and conditioner; a valuable aid in the treatment of distemper.

2 oz...........prepaid 85c   4 oz............prepaid $1.60

Sopex (soap for fleas)...........................prepaid 85c

Pulvex (powder for fleas).........................prepaid 60c

GLOVER'S DOG AND CAT MEDICINES

Prepaid

Round Worm Vermifuge—For Puppies, Dogs, Foxes and Cats.....65c

Round Worm Capsules—For Puppies, Dogs and Foxes...........65c

Tape Worm Capsules—For Puppies, Dogs and Foxes............65c

Tetrachlorethylene Capsules—For Hook Worms and Round Worms in Puppies, Dogs, Foxes and Cats.........................65c

Condition Pills—Stimulant. Digestive. Appetizer. Tonic........65c

Digestive Pills—Soothing to the Stomach and Intestines. Stimulate Digestion 65c

Laxative Pills—For Sluggish Bowels and Acute Constipation......65c

Diarrhea Mixture—To check Looseness of the Bowels from Simple Inflammations and Improper Feeding........................65c

Iron Tonic—Tonic, Appetizer. General Stimulant for Dogs and Cats 65c

Compound Sulphur Tablets—Act upon the Kidneys and Intestines..65c

Nerve Sedative—For Fits and Convulsions in Dogs and Cats.....65c

Expectorant Mixture—To Loosen the Cough and Quiet the Spasms.65c

Mange Medicine—For Superficial Mange and a Local Application for Eczema 65c

Kennel and Flea Soap—A Bath Soap for the Coat. Kills Fleas and Lice. Promotes the Healing of the Sores of Mange and Eczema 30c

Medicated Soap—A cleansing Bath Soap for House Dogs. Gives a Glossy Coat. A Cleansing Soap for Minor Wounds and Injuries 30c

Cresol Disinfectant—Antiseptic. Germicide. Insecticide. Deodorant. For the Dog, Household, Kennel and Farm..............75c

Flea and Insect Powder—100% Pyrethrum Flowers. Kills Fleas and Lice on Dogs, Cats, Farm Animals, Poultry. Used in the Household to Kill Ants, Roaches, Water Bugs and Bed Bugs..60c

Canker Wash—For the Ears of Dogs and Cats...................65c

Eye Lotion and Eye Wash Powder (Combination Package)—For Minor Injuries, Inflammations and Catarrhal Conditions of the Eye and Eyelids. For Dogs and Cats......................65c

Antiseptic Mouth Wash—For Sore Mouth and Tongue. Inflamed Gums in Dogs and Cats...................................65c

Liniment—For Muscle Soreness, Stiffness and Sprains of Dogs. A strong Liniment of even greater usefulness to Man..........65c

Sore Foot Medicine—For Dogs. Specially recommended for Hunting Dogs and for Sled Dogs of the North...................65c

BOOKS

"Feathered Pets, Their Care in Health and Disease" (illustrated), each 35c. Postpaid, 38c.

"Canary Breeding and Training" (illustrated), 35c. Postpaid, 38c.

"Canaries and Other Cage Birds" (illustrated), each 35c. Postpaid, 38c

"Parrots and Other Talking Birds" (illustrated), 35c. Postpaid, 38c.

"Aquaria," illustrated book on goldfish and other aquarium fish, 25c. Postpaid, 28c.

BIRD SEED, FOOD AND MEDICINE

See Testimonials on Pages 58 and 59.

We make a specialty of different kinds of Bird Food, Medicines and imported Bird Seed of best quality. The seed, being cleansed by machinery, is absolutely free of dust and dirt, and properly mixed, suitable for each particular kind of bird. We advise everyone loving his bird, not to buy any seed which is not put up by a well known Bird Fancier, as it requires long experience and study of the nature of birds in order to know what is becoming to them, and for this reason not everyone is able to put up proper seed. Our prices are not higher than common seed, and there is no reason why you should not buy the best and healthiest seed to be gotten for your bird, instead of the poor qualities put on the market under the common name of "Mixed Bird Seed," of which most of them are directly injurious to birds.

Our different kinds of seed and food are open to the market, and every package is guaranteed. We put them up in nice cartons and sell them to the trade at prices which allow the retail dealer handling them a fair profit. We advise all lovers of birds, if they don't find our preparations at their respective druggist or grocer, to request them to keep them in stock, and refuse all other mixtures offered to them as being "just as good." It will be to your own interest, because birds which are fed on seed and food put up by us will always stay in perfect health and good plumage, and if singers, full in song all the year round and will live much longer.

If our preparations are not handled in your town, you will oblige us by sending the names of a few reliable druggists, so we can make arrangements with one of them to carry a full line in stock.

Each Carton must bear this Registered Trade Mark:

None genuine without it.

MAX GEISLER BIRD CO., OMAHA, NEB. AND NEW YORK CITY

NOTICE

Small shipments up to about 3 lbs. are cheaper by Parcel Post and charges must be **prepaid**, while heavier shipments are cheaper by Express and can be sent charges **collect**.

For instance, a 10-lb. package of Seed or Food costs by **Express** to New York or Philadelphia 64c; by Parcel Post 83c, to Chicago by Express 47c; by Parcel Post 45c.

INSURANCE AGAINST LOSS OR DAMAGE

Shipments by Parcel Post can be insured for 5 cents extra against loss, but never against damage. But, if you will send us 10 cents extra with your order, we will insure your Parcel Post shipments against loss as well as damage. Shipments by Express do not need any insurance for the reason that the express company is responsible for the loss or damage of the packages.

Max Geisler's Genuine Imported "Roller" Seed. A scientifically balanced food for all kinds of Canaries, especially German Roller Canaries. The only food that will keep Canaries in perfect health and singing condition the year round. Valuable directions on each box.

		Prepaid
Per carton ....$ .25		$ .35
2 cartons		.65
Per dozen cartons........ 2.50		

Max Geisler's Pure Egg Bird Biscuit. Same preparation as the Canary Breeders in Germany are using. It will keep birds in health and song. A box will last one bird eight weeks. Directions on box.

Per carton	.20	.23
2 cartons		.45
Per dozen cartons................................	2.00	

Max Geisler's Mixed Parrot Seed. The only properly mixed seed to feed Parrots with, in order to keep them in good health and plumage. Full and valuable directions on the care of Parrots on each box.

Per carton	.25	.35
2 cartons		.65
Per dozen cartons................................	2.50	

Max Geisler's Prepared Corn, for Parrots, to be given in addition to the seed.

Per carton	.15	.30
3 cartons		.75
Per dozen cartons................................	1.50	

Max Geisler's Parrot Biscuit, an additional food, excellent for old and young Parrots, to keep them in good health and plumage. One box, if fed daily, will last a Parrot 48 days. Directions on box.

Per carton	.25	.40
2 cartons		.75
Per dozen cartons................................	2.50	

Max Geisler's Prepared Food for Baby Parrots. The only
   proper food for baby parrots which are too young yet
   to eat seed.   Prepaid
   Per carton ....$ .20 $ .30
   Per dozen cartons................................... 2.00

Max Geisler's "Health Food" for Parrots. The greatest
   improved food for Parrots, to be fed in addition to the
   seed. It contains **vegetable nourishment,** same as
   Parrots consume in their liberty and which is the
   only means by which their system is furnished with
   healthy blood. Wonderful how Parrots will improve
   in health when fed regularly on this food. A trial will
   convince you.
   Per carton .... .25   **.35**
   3 cartons 1.00
   Per dozen cartons.............................. 2.50

Max Geisler's "Health Food" for Canaries, Redbirds,
   Mockingbirds, and all other seed-eating and soft-billed
   cage birds. Contains the same vegetable nourishment
   as foregoing preparation.
   Per carton .... .20   .23
   2 cartons 45
   Per dozen cartons.............................. 2.00

Max Geisler's Prepared Mockingbird Food, put up in tin
   cans, with directions. We guarantee this to be the
   best, most natural and healthiest prepared food of its
   kind on the market. Try it and you will use no other
   in future.
   Per tin .... .30   .40
   Per dozen tins.................................... 3.00

Max Geisler's Prepared Nightingale Food, put up in tin
   cans. The purest and richest food for small soft-billed
   birds such as Nightingales, Robins, Blackcaps, etc.
   Will keep in any climate.
   Per tin .... .40   .50
   Per dozen tins.................................... 4.00

Max Geisler's Prepared Bird Grit. It is prepared to
   prevent birds from getting vermine of any kind and
   will also add wonderfully to their digestion.
   Per carton .... .15   .30
   3 cartons 85
   Per dozen cartons.............................. 1.50

Max Geisler's Medicated Bird Biscuit. A combination of
   food and medicine. It is easy digestible and can be
   given to the most delicate bird. It will strengthen
   weak birds and give new life and vigor to sick birds.
   Per carton .... .25   .28
   2 cartons 55
   Per dozen cartons................................. 2.35

Max Geisler's Song and Moulting Food for birds which
   are shedding feathers out of season and have stopped
   singing.
   Per carton .... .15   .18
   2 cartons 35
   Per dozen cartons.............................. 1.50

Max Geisler's Vegetable Extract, to be added to the drinking water, it should be given every spring and during moulting season. It is the best blood tonic and blood producer in existence. No bird should be without it.

		Prepaid
Per vial	.30	.35
Per dozen vials..................................	3.00	

Max Geisler's Mite Powder (non-poisonous) to be blown under feathers of the bird.

Per package	.10	.12
Per dozen packages..............................	1.00	

Max Geisler's Parrot Spray. Will cure Parrots of the habit of destroying their plumage by biting off feathers.

Per bottle	.50	.65
Per dozen bottles................................	5.00	

Max Geisler's Prepared Fish Food. A suitable food for Goldfish, etc. Full directions on each box on the proper care of Goldfish and the management of an Aquarium.

Per box	.15	.17
Per three boxes..................................		.45
Per dozen boxes................................	1.50	

Max Geisler's Daphnia Fish Food. 100% natural, consists only of pure dried water insects...Best for all kinds of Aquarium Fish.

Per tin	.15	.17
Per 3 tins		.45

Max Geisler's Aquarium Cement. Put up in tins which will make 2½ pounds of best cement.

Per tin	.25	.35
Per dozen tins...................................	2.50	

Max Geisler's Bird Tonics.

Per dozen bottles, assorted..........................$3.00

Treatment A. (Song Restorer). For birds which have lost their voice from cold, etc....................

	.30	$ .40
3 bottles for....................................		1.15

Treatment B. (Digestive Trouble). For birds which have lost their appetite, when bowels are out of order, etc....................................

	.30	.40
3 bottles for....................................		1.15

Treatment C. (Cold). For birds which are breathing hard, coughing, etc................................

	.30	.40
3 bottles for....................................		1.15

Treatment D. (General Tonic). For birds which are puffed and are apparently sick, without showing symptoms of a certain disease....................

	.30	.40
3 bottles for....................................		1.15

Max Geisler's Parrot Tonic, a medicine which is especially prepared for Parrots. Unexcelled for young Parrots as it cures catarrh, which most of them become affected with.

Per bottle	.30	.40
3 bottles for....................................		1.15

Max Geisler's Canary Food Outfit, a scientifically balanced assortment of six necessary food articles that will keep all kinds of canaries in song and health the year round, indispensable for those who wish to start feeding their canaries correctly. Per outfit....................80c Prepaid....$1.00

BIRD SEED AND FOOD IN BULK

	Pound	Prepaid 1 lb.	Prepaid 3 lbs.
Properly mixed Seed for Shell Paroquets, etc........	$ .20	$ .30	$ .80
Properly mixed seed for small Finches..............	.20	.30	.80
Properly mixed Seed for Goldfinches, and Seed for all other birds. When ordering state what kind bird it is to be used for........................	.20	.30	.80
Imported German Summer Rape, best selected quality	.25	.35	1.15
Imported Sicily Canary	.15	.25	.70
Imported Russian Hemp	.15	.25	.70
Hulled Oats	.15	.25	.70
American Sunflower	.15	.25	.65
Imported German White Millet.....................	.20	.30	.85
Imported German Yellow Millet....................	.15	.25	.70
Imported German Blue Maw.......................	.35	.45	1.35
Mexican Nuts, for Parrots........................	.40	.50	1.40
Unhulled Rice	.20	.30	.80

Dried Ant Eggs..........................15c per oz.

Meal Worms, 100 for 35c, prepaid 45c; 1,000 for $2.50, prepaid for $2.75

Cuttlefish, each ....5c; prepaid 10c

---

SOMETHING ABOUT SICK BIRDS

There are numerous bird medicines put up, generally under the name of "Bird Tonic," which are claimed to cure all diseases of Birds. People with common sense will admit that this is impossible.

We have put up special Tonics for each occasion and named them, respectively "Treatment A, B, C, D," etc.

It will be advisable for everyone who really loves his bird to keep a full line of these medicines on hand, for the sooner you treat a sick bird the more chance you have to cure him. Certain diseases if settled too far into the system become incurable. Follow this advice and it may probably be the cause of saving the life of your bird. If you should not be successful in treating your bird and you wish to correspond with us regarding him, we will be glad to advise you to the best of our ability free of charge, and if any special medicine is required we shall only charge for the same the actual cost, which will be from 15c to 50c. We have cured many hundreds of birds this way, and have saved many a one already given up by its owner.

When writing in regard to a sick bird, state the following: (a) Kind and age of bird. (b) What kind of seed or food you have been feeding him (mail a small sample of it if possible) and how you have been taking care of him. (c) Take the bird in your hand and examine if his breast is full and fleshy or if sharp and bony. (d) Describe the droppings, their color and condition, and send some of it, wrapped in wax paper with your letter. (e) State since when sick, and describe all visible symptoms of the disease. (f) State if cage is placed close to a window or not. We will answer by return mail and send full instructions for treatment, and will also send the proper medicine, if remittance accompanies letter.

One Warning: Among all diseases, the most met with in birds are those of the "Respiratory Organs." They are commonly known as "Colds." It is an old saying (and is still recommended by many bird dealers nowadays), that the removal of the horny scale which will form on the point of the tongue, by peeling or cutting off with a knife, will cure the disease. It should be hardly necessary to mention that this is only a cruel, unnecessary torture to the poor bird, as it is of no beneficial effect whatever. The dry, hard point of the tongue is natural, caused by the inner heat of the sick bird, and will disappear by itself as soon as the body has regained its normal temperature.

For birds which have lost their song from cold, over-singing or unfinished shedding, our Tonic A (Song Restorer), price 30c, prepaid 40c, and our "Song and Moulting Food," 15c, or 18c prepaid, will be a sure remedy.

What Our Patrons Have to Say About Our Bird Preparations

Mrs. William Ellis, 42 John street, Williamantic, Ct., writes: "Please send me Roller Seed, Pure Egg Bird Biscuit and Moulting Food. I think that your Bird Foods are fine. My bird is a wonderful singer, he sings the whole year round even when he is moulting. I feed him your Song and Moulting Food when he first starts to moult and he does not lose his song."

Mrs. Mallicoat, Tarkio, Mo., writes: "My singer for which I obtained your advice and remedy a few weeks ago is fine and in good health now. New feathers have come in and you would never know his face and head had been bald. He sings beautifully."

Mrs. Gilbert Hogue, 216 Keystone, avenue, Cresson, Pa., writes: "Write and tell me how you sell Max Geisler's Roller Bird Seed. After using one box my bird began to sing, then I tried our drug store here, also asked them to send and get me the seed. The one box I got was sent direct from your company."

Mrs. Powell Burch, De Queen, Ark., writes: "Have one German Roller singer and I am delighted with the improvement in his voice since using your products."

Mrs. R. T. Frambes, 2320 Fairview avenue, Mt. Penn, Reading, Penn., writes: "Please send me one package Song and Moulting Food. I am so glad to tell you that my canary has continued singing through the moulting season. I attribute it all to Max Geisler's Bird Food and recommend it whenever I can."

Mrs. F. E. Brown, 1217 Fannie, Wichita, Kansas, writes: "Have used your Seed for some time. Last summer my bird laid three eggs. Hatched eggs and have raised three birds. Have used only your seed. Two singers which started to sing at three weeks old."

George W. Church, 143 N. Robinson street, Philadelphia, Pa., writes: "Enclosed find $1.25 for a box of your "Canary Food Outfit" marked at a dollar. Our bird is doing fine and I passed on the tonic to my mother at Baltimore and last reports say it is doing fine."

Mrs. Settie Goodwin, Star Route, Payette, Idaho, writes: "I had been using another brand of Bird Seed, but find the Max Geisler Roller Seed so much better and my birds consumed every seed."

Mrs. B. G. Board, Milan, Mo., writes: "Please send me a package of Song and Moulting Food. Have never been without this food for my birds since I first bought them and certainly do not want to as I think it is the most help while shedding feathers."

Mrs. C. L. Odell, 1910 Dartmouth avenue, Bessemer, Ala., writes: "Bird stops singing after moulting. I had given him every attention, one whole pantry shelf being filled with different things I have gotten for him, still he would not sing. Early this spring, I saw your Seed advertisement and I wrote for a package of Seed. At the end of three weeks my little "beauty" was singing joyously again. When seed gave out, thinking he was entirely himself again and not knowing of your Seed being handled anywhere in this district I returned to use of other seed. At the end of several weeks the little bird was silent again, beautiful and well, but no song. I am enclosing the required 35c for a package of your Roller Seed and intend never again to use any other."

Mrs. S. G. Story, 6607 29th avenue, Kenosha, Wis., writes: "I have been a user of your bird products since the middle of last December and I must say that they are fine. My bird hadn't sung for 6 months and the Seed and Pure Egg Biscuit returned his voice in a very short time. I am also very much pleased to find that the bald spot on the back of his head is nearly gone and I have had him 3 years and he was like that when I got him, so you see it is doing remarkable for my bird by sending for your bird products. I recommend it and it is by doing so that I have given away my book and wish another sent."

Mrs. H. S. Jaquiss, Cincinnati, Iowa, writes: "I have 5 spring birds, been feeding your Bird Biscuit to my young birds and the parent birds and everyone remarks what nice birds and what large birds and I feel I can lay it all to Bird Biscuit and Health Food."

Mrs. H. Agrell, 224 N. 22nd St., Billings, Mont., writes: "I have been using your seed and Remedies, find they are very good for any kind of bird. I had a Roller off of song for a year. I finally decided to try your Seed and Extract; it did wonders. He is singing day and night now. Is fat and feels fine, his plumage is the prettiest I ever saw it, so slick and glossy. Also I would like to mention your A, B, C and D remedies, I used also they are all you claim of them and then some. I will always be glad to recommend your supplies to anyone."

Mrs. E. G. Schueller, Palisade, Colorado, writes: "I use your Seeds and I have gotten several others to using them. I wouldn't feed my birds any other when I can get your seeds, biscuits and other foods for my birds. My bird is a beautiful singer. He is singing now while I am writing; we sure love him. Am sorry I haven't written before but I live on a fruit ranch and have been busy, etc."

THE CANARY

Full Directions How to Feed and Take Care of Canaries

To keep canaries in perfect health and song it is absolutely necessary that the following instructions be strictly observed: Feed nothing but Geisler's Genuine "Roller" Seed, which are composed of the finest genuine Imported Summer Rape, with best quality Cicily Canary Seed and other seeds, scientifically mixed in the proper proportions to make a perfect balanced food. Too much stress cannot be laid on the importance of this point, for your Canary's voice as well as health depends on his food. The quality, purity, and cleanliness of the seed especially the Rape Seed, determine whether his voice will keep its soft, sweet quality, with a great variety of full mellodious notes, or whether it will become harsh and loud and he will drop one note after another until he finally stops singing altogether. American and other Cheap Rape is directly harmful and dangerous. I import all my own seed and absolutely guarantee that this package contains the best quality of Genuine Imported Summer Rape which money can buy. Test it for yourself—chew a few of the Rape Seeds (they are the small dark seeds) and note their mild, rather sweet, very agreeable taste, the sign of good Rape. Then compare this with the sharp, tongue-burning, even bitter taste of the Rape from any ordinary bird seed.

Let the bird eat as much seed as he wants, and fill his cup after cleaning it thoroughly with fresh seed every morning. Give him one-eighth of a cake of "Max Geisler's Maizena Bird Biscuit" three times a week and one-half teaspoonful of "Max Geisler's Health Food for Canaries" once a week. On the alternate days give a little lettuce as long as obtainable, or in its place a piece of ripe apple or boiled carrot, a piece as large as a small walnut, but do not let any unconsumed pieces remain in the cage over night. Fresh, but not cold drinking water (same temperature as room is best) should be given every day after first cleaning the cup thoroughly. Let him have a bath during the summer daily and during the cold season (lukewarm) twice a week. Keep the bottom of the cage covered with "Max Geisler's Prepared Bird Grit," which will not only keep his feet in good condition and prevent the bird from getting vermins, but it will also be beneficial for his digestion. Clean the cage at least twice a week. Have a piece of cuttlefish bone in the cage all the time. When the bird begins to shed feathers, give him daily on top of the seed one-half teaspoonful of "Max Geisler's Song and Moulting Food," and if you wish to assist your bird in getting through this critical period of a bird's life quickly and safely add to his drinking water "Max Geisler's Vegetable Extract" until he has finished his moult. Keep him in a room of as even temperature as possible (68 to 70 degrees F). Never place your bird so he can see another one, especially not during the mating season (February to June) or else he will oversing himself, become hoarse and stop singing, which will also occur if you allow your bird to sing until late at night.

Never hang the cage above the gas, if any, and never too close to a fire, neither too close to a window, especially not in winter, as there is always more or less draught, which will cause your bird to lose his voice. Of course on warm, pleasant days during the summer you can hang his cage at the open window, providing there is no door or other window open on opposite side of the room, as this would cause draught, or you may even put him outside, if well protected from the wind. Let him have a sun bath for an hour every morning, but cover half of the cage so that he can move out of the sun if he wants to. A Roller, if in good condition, should be singing all the year around, except during the mounting season (July and August). Should he stop singing any length of time outside of the moulting season give him immediately "Max Geisler's Bird Tonic A" (Song Restorer) in his drinking water as per printed directions on the bottle. Should he act dumpish (feathers puffed up, appetite poor, etc.) use "Max Geisler's Bird Tonic D." It is advisable to have a bottle of each on hand all the time; it may save you a lot of trouble. By following these directions strictly you will be able to enjoy the song of your bird for many years.

Although "Max Geisler's Imported Roller Seed" is especially prepared for Andreasberg Roller Canaries, it can also be fed to any other kind of Canaries by making them gradually used to it, and by so doing you will soon note a wonderful improvement in your bird's voice.

THE PARROT

Full Directions How to Feed and Take Care of Parrots

Of all Parrots kept in captivity, there will be, we claim, at least ninety out of every hundred which, regarding food, are treated entirely wrong. Not on account of carelessness of the owner, but simply because he does not know any better. As a rule a Parrot, when not fed properly, will take sick within a short time, but we also know cases where Parrots seemed to appear well for years, until all at once "Polly" was sick. Bowel troubles, which cause many Parrots' death, self-destroying of plumage by biting off feathers (caused by feeding bones, or potatoes with gravy, or other greasy and unnatural food), and other sicknesses will and are bound to show up sooner or later. Therefore, we earnestly warn all Parrot owners, if they did not take proper care of their pets so far, not to run any further risks by letting it go the old way; but to observe the following rules, which are given by a Bird Fancier of thirty years' experience, and which he has found to be the best to keep Parrots perfect in health and good in plumage all the time. It is just as much trouble to feed a Parrot right as it is to feed him wrong.

The principal food of a full-grown Parrot should be "SEED"—

best Russian Hemp, Russian Sunflower, Sicily Canary, Unhulled Rice, Mexican Black Corn and Nuts, of the very best quality, mixed in proper proportion, as contained in Max Geisler's "Mixed Parrot Seed." Fill the seed-cup with fresh seed every day and allow him to eat of it as much as he wants. Every morning let him have one-fourth cake (dry) of Max Geisler's "Parrot Biscuit." (One box will last one Parrot seven weeks.) This is very nourishing and healthy, because it contains ingredients that the Parrot get in his wild state. In the afternoon fill the other cup half with water, to which you have added some of Max Geisler's "Vegetable Extract," but never use ice cold water; boiled water of same temperature as room is best. Only leave the water in for ten minutes; this is sufficient. One-half hour later give in same cup, two teaspoonsfuls of Max Geisler's "Health Food" for Parrots (slightly moistened as per directions on box). Toward evening offer him another drink of water. Every other day give him some sweet, ripe fruit, such as apples, pears, bananas, etc., a piece as big as a small chicken egg. But if the bowels should become too loose stop feeding fruit for several days. Twice a week give a tablespoonful of Max Geisler's "Parrot Corn," once a week a small piece of Cuttlefish bone. Clean, dry gravel, free from dust, should be put in the bottom of the cage fresh every day. It will favor digestion and gives the Parrot a chance to clean his feet and plumage. Clean the cage every evening and remove all food over night. As Parrots very seldom go into a bathing dish, it is advisable to sprinkle him with lukewarm water about twice a week or oftener in summer, once every week in winter, but care should be taken that he can get dry afterwards in a warm place. If you add a few drops of Max Geisler's "Parrot Spray" to the water, it will keep his plumage in a beautiful condition all the year around. Keep the Parrot in a room of even temperature, where no draught will strike him; allow him during warm weather as much fresh air as possible, and give him once in a while a small branch of some kind of a fruit tree to gnaw on, which is very healthy.

Young Parrots require the same care, with the only difference that as long as they do not eat seed yet, they must have soft food, therefore they ought to get Max Geisler's "Prepared Food for Baby Parrots," mixed with a teaspoonful of Max Geisler's "Health Food" (soaked) twice a day, morning and afternoon, and in the time between our "Prepared Corn for Parrots," slightly boiled as per directions on box and mixed with "Health Food."

By following these rules your Parrot will remain in perfect health all the time and will repay your trouble by a nice appearance and better inclination to talk.

We especially warn against the old style of feeding Parrots, namely, "bread or crackers" soaked in coffee." This or any other "sop" is bound to derange the bowels, until the stomach becomes so weak that it cannot digest the food any more, besides the "caffein" contained in the coffee is poisonous.

THE SHAMA THRUSH

Full Directions How to Feed and Take Care of Shama Thrushes and Other Soft Billed Birds of Same Size

Take four heaping teaspoonfuls of "Max Geisler's Prepared Mocking Bird Food," which is about the right amount for one day's ration for a Shama or Mocking Bird or a bird of same size, and mix this with about two heaping teaspoonfuls of coarse, grated, raw carrot. If the carrot should be too juicy, use a little less; if too dry, a little more of it. To be right the food should be light and loose, therefore never squeeze it together when mixing, as this would make it bulky and unfit to eat. Always prepare each day's ration fresh, so as to prevent it from becoming sour. Every third day use a change some grated hard boiled egg instead of the carrot, to mix with the food, and give on these days a small piece of lettuce between the wire of the cage, or if lettuce is not obtainable a small piece of ripe fruit, according to season. Occasionally add a few soaked currants or small raisins to the food. If you wish to keep your bird in excellent condition and in full song, you must give him a liberal supply of live meal worms daily. (We send 100 meal worms for 45c, postpaid.) Shama Thrushes and birds of similar size should receive at least five to ten a day, but the double quantity during moulting season. When the bird is shedding feathers, give him in his drinking water "Max Geisler's Vegetable Extract," which will greatly assist him in going through this critical period of a bird's life with safety. Let the drinking water always be fresh, but never too cold. Give a fresh supply every day, during hot weather twice a day, and pay strict attention to the cleanliness of the cups, food as well as water cups. Allow him a bath every day or at least every other day during the warm season, and twice a week during the winter months. Use lukewarm water on chilly and cold days. Let the bird have as much fresh air as possible during warm weather, and always keep the cage in a very light place, in a room of even temperature 68 to 70 degrees F., well protected from draughts. Let him enjoy a sun bath for an hour during the forenoon, but have half of his cage shaded so he may move out of the sun at leisure. Never hang the cage during the winter months too close to the window, especially not over night. Keep the bottom of the cage well covered with "Max Geisler's Prepared Bird Gravel," which will not only keep his feet in good condition and prevent him from getting vermins, but will also be beneficial to his digestion. The cage of soft-billed birds should be cleaned every day. Never try to keep Shama Thrushes or Mocking Birds in too small a cage, as they will never do well for any length of time. 12x20 inches and 18 inches height should be the smallest size. If the bird should appear dumpish (feathers puffed up, appetite poor), give without delay for one time only, three meal worms dipped in olive oil, and in his drinking water "Max Geisler's Bird Tonic D." To have a bottle of the latter always on hand all the time, mav save you a lot of trouble, probably the life of your pet.

THE NIGHTINGALE

And Other Soft Billed Birds of Same Size

Should receive the same care as described for the Shama Thrush, with the only difference that they must be fed on "Max Geisler's Prepared Nightingale Food."

THE GOLDFISH

Goldfish should be fed once a day at a regular hour. The quantity given should not exceed what they will consume within ten minutes. You may count about one-eighth of a sheet for a fish of medium size. Once or twice a week they should be fed on Daphnia, of which this box contains a proportional quantity. Unconsumed food should be removed from the water as soon as possible.

Directions Regarding the Management of the Aquarium

Never overstock an Aquarium. Allow not more than two Goldfish, 2 to 3 inches in size, to each gallon of water, or less fish in average if same are larger. The best temperature for the water is about 60 degrees Fahrenheit. Never try to keep Goldfish without a sufficient quantity of Aquatic Plants. These, by growing, give "oxygen" to the water, a necessity for the good health of the fish. "Cabomba Palustris" is the best plant for this purpose. A bunch of it (25c prepaid by mail) is sufficient to keep the water for six medium fish in healthy condition. The water of an aquarium properly stocked with these plants would not need to be changed for months, while otherwise it requires changing every day in summer, or twice a week in winter. But always change immediately if the fish come frequently to the top of the water to breathe. If a Goldfish appears sickly place him for a minute or two in salt water to the strength of a heaping teaspoonful of salt to a quart of water, but remove immediately if he should turn on his side. Place the aquarium where the full light will strike it and have the bottom of it covered with coarse gravel.